Team Spirit

THE SACRAMENTO KINGS

BY

MARK STEWART

Content Consultant
Matt Zeysing
Historian and Archivist
The Naismith Memorial Basketball Hall of Fame

NORWOOD HOUSE PRESS

CHICAGO, ILLINOIS

Norwood House Press
P.O. Box 316598
Chicago, Illinois 60631

For information regarding Norwood House Press, please visit our website at:
www.norwoodhousepress.com or call 866-565-2900.

All photos courtesy of Getty Images except the following:
Capital Cards (6, 18), TCMA, Inc. (7, 34 right),
Black Book Partners Archive (9, 36), Bowman Gum Co. (14, 19, 20, 40 top),
General Mills, Inc. (16), Complete Sports Publications, Inc. (21),
Topps, Inc. (22, 28, 30, 35 top left & right, 39, 40 bottom, 41 top),
Kahn's Wieners (31), The Star Co. (34 left, 43),
Allstar Arena Entertainment (37), Author's Collection (41 left), Matt Richman (48)
Cover Photo: Rocky Widner/Getty Images
Special thanks to Topps, Inc.

Editor: Mike Kennedy
Designer: Ron Jaffe
Project Management: Black Book Partners, LLC.
Research: Joshua Zaffos

Special thanks to Cathy Betts

Library of Congress Cataloging-in-Publication Data

Stewart, Mark, 1960-
    The Sacramento Kings / by Mark Stewart ; content consultant, Matt
Zeysing.
       p. cm. -- (Team spirit)
    Includes bibliographical references and index.
    Summary: "Presents the history and accomplishments of the Sacramento
Kings basketball team. Includes highlights of players, coaches, and awards,
quotes, timelines, maps, glossary and websites"--Provided by publisher.
    ISBN-13: 978-1-59953-285-1 (library edition : alk. paper)
    ISBN-10: 1-59953-285-9 (library edition : alk. paper) 1. Sacramento
Kings (Basketball team)--History--Juvenile literature. I. Zeysing, Matt.
II. Title.
    GV885.52.S24S33 2009
    796.323'640979454--dc22
                                                        2008039806

COVER PHOTO: The Kings celebrate a good play during a 2007–08 game.

Table of Contents

SPORTS WORDS & VOCABULARY WORDS: In this book, you will find many words that are new to you. You may also see familiar words used in new ways. The glossary on page 46 gives the meanings of basketball words, as well as "everyday" words that have special basketball meanings. These words appear in **bold type** throughout the book. The glossary on page 47 gives the meanings of vocabulary words that are not related to basketball. They appear in ***bold italic type*** throughout the book.

BASKETBALL SEASONS: Because each basketball season begins late in one year and ends early in the next, seasons are not named after years. Instead, they are written out as two years separated by a dash, for example 1944–45 or 2005–06.

Meet the Kings

The story of **professional** basketball began in the East. Little by little, the sport spread west—much like people living in the United States. The Sacramento Kings have followed a similar path. They began their journey in New York and then moved across the heartland. They now call California their home.

The Kings changed their name along the way. They were once called the Royals. Both names fit the team very well, because it has always had plenty of star power. Indeed, some of basketball's top performers have played for the club.

This book tells the story of the Kings. They have made history in five different cities, but their story is far from over. The team is always searching for ways to improve and always keeps its eye on the future. Sacramento fans are hungrier than ever for a championship contender. If the Kings have their way, they will serve up that title in style.

Kevin Martin rises high for a shot during a 2007–08 game. He joined the team in 2004 and soon became a star.

Way Back When

The Kings trace their roots back to the earliest days of basketball. During the 1920s, a young businessman named Les Harrison began supporting teams in Rochester, New York. By the early 1940s, Harrison was fielding one of the country's best teams. It starred Paul Nowak and Al Cervi. In 1945, Harrison's team joined the **National Basketball League (NBL)**. The NBL later joined forces with the **Basketball Association of America (BAA)** to become the **National Basketball Association (NBA)**.

Harrison named his team the Royals and coached it until 1955. Rochester won the NBL Championship in 1945–46 and again in 1946–47. The league made a new rule that second year. The team with the best record (not the winner of the **playoffs**!) would be declared the champion. Even though the Royals lost to the Chicago American Gears in the playoffs, they won the league title because they had the most wins during the season.

Rochester joined the BAA in 1948–49, the season before the NBA formed. Bob Davies, Red Holzman, and Bobby Wanzer gave the team three top guards. Arnie Risen, Arnie Johnson, and Jack Coleman were the Royals' best big men. In 1950–51, that group led Rochester to the NBA Championship.

The Royals moved to Cincinnati, Ohio for the 1957–58 season. Their star was Oscar Robertson, a 6′ 5″ guard who was impossible to stop. Robertson was a great shooter, passer, and rebounder. He was also a rugged defensive player. When he teamed with center Wayne Embry and forwards Jack Twyman and Jerry Lucas, no one wanted to play against Cincinnati.

Unfortunately for the Royals, they were in the same **division** as powerful teams from Boston and Philadelphia. The Royals often struggled in the regular season and the playoffs. By the 1970s, fans in Cincinnati had grown tired of rooting for the Royals. In 1972, the team moved west. The Royals split their games between Omaha, Nebraska and Kansas City, Missouri. Since Kansas City already had a baseball team called the Royals, the team changed its name to the Kings.

The Kings had some excellent players in the 1970s. Their best was Nate "Tiny" Archibald. He was a good shooter and passer—and the

LEFT: Les Harrison, the team's first owner.   **ABOVE**: Oscar Robertson, who many consider the best player in team history.

quickest player in the NBA. During the 1972–73 season, Archibald

became the first player to lead the league in points and **assists**! Tiny's teammates included Sam Lacey, Jimmy Walker, Tom Van Arsdale, and Scott Wedman. Lacey was a favorite of the fans. He was a superb passer who scored many of his points on bank shots and hook shots.

In 1985–86, the Kings continued their move west, when they landed in Sacramento, the capital of California. Several talented players wore the Sacramento uniform in the years that followed, including Otis Thorpe, Reggie Theus, Wayman Tisdale, Lionel Simmons, and Brian Grant. No one was better than Mitch Richmond, a 6′ 5″ guard who reminded many fans of Oscar Robertson. Richmond had a deadly outside shot and a big body, which he used to overpower smaller guards.

The Kings played more than a *decade* in Sacramento without a winning record. Still, the fans cheered them on. Thanks to this great support, the team was hard to beat on its home court. In 1998, Sacramento hired Rick Adelman to run the team. By 2000, the Kings were back on the winning track.

LEFT: Mitch Richmond brings the ball up the court. He followed in the footsteps of Oscar Robertson. **ABOVE**: Nate Archibald, whose nickname was "Tiny."

The Team Today

In the early years of the 21st *century*, the Kings built a new club with skill and talent at every position. Sacramento traded for young stars Chris Webber and Mike Bibby. The team also gave important jobs to **role players** such as Bobby Jackson, Doug Christie, and Scot Pollard. The Kings signed top international players as well, including Peja Stojakovic, Hedo Turkgolu, and Vlade Divac.

In 2001–02, the Kings won 61 games. No team in the NBA had a better record. They faced Kobe Bryant, Shaquille O'Neal, and the Los Angeles Lakers in the **Western Conference Finals**. It was a thrilling series that lasted seven games. The Kings outplayed the Lakers and led in the final moments of Game 7. Somehow, the Lakers pulled even and won in **overtime**.

In the years that followed, the Kings fell short of their goal to reach the NBA Finals. However, they set a standard of excellence for the future. New stars such as Kevin Martin and Spencer Hawes know they have a great *tradition* to *uphold*.

Kevin Martin, Mikki Moore, and Beno Udrih celebrate a great play during the 2007–08 season.

Home Court

During the team's history, it has made its home in many different places. The first home court of the Rochester Royals was the Edgerton Park Arena. The building had once served as a school for troubled boys.

During its years in Ohio, the team played in Cincinnati Gardens. That arena looked just like the famous Maple Leaf Gardens in Toronto, Canada. The Kings used three different arenas when they moved to Kansas City and Omaha.

The Kings opened a fantastic new arena in Sacramento in 1988. They now share it with the Monarchs of the **Women's National Basketball Association (WNBA)**. The arena is famous for its wooden floors. When the fans stomp their feet, it makes a lot of noise. This helps give the Kings a great homecourt advantage. No NBA team enjoys traveling to Sacramento for a game.

 BY THE NUMBERS

- *The Kings' arena has 17,317 seats for basketball.*
- *The arena cost $40 million to build in the 1980s.*
- *The arena is the smallest in the NBA and has the second-fewest number of seats.*

The crowd gets loud before a 2007–08 game at the Kings' arena.

Dressed for Success

The Kings went by several different names in their early days. In the 1940s, they were named after one company that sold fruits and vegetables, and another that made liquor. When the team joined the NBL in 1946, Les Harrison decided it was time for a permanent name. A contest was held among Rochester sports fans. A teenage fan won with the entry of Royals. The team kept this name during its years in Rochester and Cincinnati. In 1972, the team became the Kings after its move west.

All along, the team's *logo* has used the points of a crown. In Cincinnati, the Royals had a fun logo. It featured a basketball-shaped head wearing a crown.

Blue and white (and later red) were the team's main colors until the 1994–95 season. That year, the Kings switched to a more modern uniform design that used purple as the main color. Throughout history, purple has been a popular color for kings. Sacramento also uses silver and black in its uniform and logo.

Arnie Johnson models the Royals uniform from the days when the team played in Rochester.

UNIFORM BASICS

The basketball uniform is very simple. It consists of a roomy top and baggy shorts.

- The top hangs from the shoulders, with big "scoops" for the arms and neck. This style has not changed much over the years.

- Shorts, however, have changed a lot. They used to be very short, so players could move their legs freely. In the last 20 years, shorts have actually gotten longer and much baggier.

Basketball uniforms look the same as they did long ago … until you look very closely. In the old days, the shorts had belts and buckles. The tops were made of a thick cotton called "jersey," which got very heavy when players sweated. Later, uniforms were made of shiny **satin**. They may have looked great, but they did not "breathe." Players got very hot! Today, most uniforms are made of **synthetic** materials that soak up sweat and keep the body cool.

Mikki Moore wears the team's 2008–09 home uniform.

We Won!

Long before the Kings made Sacramento their home, they won championships in two professional leagues. Playing as the Rochester Royals in 1945–46, the team finished second in the NBL's Eastern Division. The Royals had an awesome starting five of

BOB DAVIES
FORWARD, ROCHESTER ROYALS

Bob Davies, Al Cervi, Red Holzman, George Glamack, and John Mahnken. To a basketball fan of that era, that **lineup** seemed like a team of **All-Stars**.

World War II had just ended when the season began. Several Royals were still in the military, so they often missed games. The team signed athletes from other sports to help out. Del Rice was a **rookie** catcher for the St. Louis Cardinals. Chuck Connors played in the **minor leagues** for the Brooklyn Dodgers. The Royals' best **substitute** was Otto Graham. A few months after the basketball season, he became the quarterback of the Cleveland Browns.

The NBL had two rounds of championship playoffs. The Royals first played the Fort Wayne Pistons. They had been NBL champions in

ABOVE: A trading card of Bob Davies.
RIGHT: Red Holzman dribbles around a defender.

1944 and 1945. The Pistons beat the Royals in the opening game. The Royals tied the series with a 58–52 victory. Rochester won again by the same score in Game 3. Glamack and Cervi were the stars of that contest. They were even better in Game 4. Glamack used his hook shot to score 23 points. Cervi played great defense and also scored 23 points. The Royals won 70–54 to reach the NBL Finals.

There they met the Sheboygan Redskins, who had the size to stop Rochester's big men. However, the Redskins could not keep up with the Royals' lightning-fast ball handlers. Rochester put on a dazzling show of passing and swept the series in three games.

The Royals were declared NBL champions again a year later, even though they lost in the playoffs to the Chicago American Gears. The team's third championship came in 1950–51. The Royals were now part of the NBA. Davies and Holzman were still in uniform—and Les Harrison still owned and coached the team—but the rest of the cast had changed.

Arnie Risen was a clever player who lined up at center for Rochester. If opponents got rough with him, **burly** Arnie Johnson would step in and take care of things. The Royals also had Bobby Wanzer and Jack Coleman. Wanzer was an excellent shooter. Coleman could rebound, shoot, and play center when Risen needed a break.

The Royals beat the Pistons in the first round of the playoffs. Next came their biggest challenge, George Mikan and the Minneapolis Lakers. The big center was the league leader in scoring and was second in rebounds. After the Lakers won the first game, Harrison urged his players to use their quickness and passing to get better shots. Against all odds, the Royals swept the final three games of the series. Now only the New York Knicks stood between them and the NBA Championship.

The series was advertised as a matchup between the league's two best **playmakers**, Davies and Dick McGuire of the Knicks. Davies was the star of the first two games, and the Royals won both easily. The series moved from Rochester to New York City. This time it was Risen who took control. He scored 27 points in a 78–71 victory.

In Game 4, Rochester built a 17-point lead. The Royals seemed to be in total command. Suddenly, the Knicks woke up. They stormed back to win by six points. New York then took the next two contests to force Game 7 in Rochester. It was exciting from start to finish. The Royals grabbed the lead in the first quarter, but the Knicks kept the score close. New York tied the game in the fourth quarter and then moved ahead.

Risen and Sweetwater Clifton of the Knicks had been battling all game long. Clifton was called for his sixth foul and sent to the Knicks' bench. Risen immediately scored three points to give the Royals the lead again. With Rochester ahead 77–74, Holzman dribbled in circles as the clock ran down. He then fired a pass to Coleman who scored a basket right before the final buzzer. The Royals were champs of the basketball world for the third time!

LEFT: Bobby Wanzer
ABOVE: Arnie Risen

Go-To Guys

To be a true star in the NBA, you need more than a great shot. You have to be a "go-to guy"—someone teammates trust to make the winning play when the seconds are ticking away in a big game. Fans of the Royals and Kings have had a lot to cheer about over the years, including these great stars …

THE PIONEERS

BOB DAVIES   6´ 1˝ **Guard**

• Born: 1/15/1920   • Died: 4/22/1990   • Played for Team: 1945–46 to 1954–55

Bob Davies was a wonderful team leader and also a favorite of the fans. He was the first player to use the behind-the-back dribble. When the NBA celebrated its 25th anniversary, Davies was named one of the league's 10 greatest players.

BOBBY WANZER   6´ 0˝ **Guard**

• Born: 6/4/1921   • Played for Team: 1947–48 to 1956–57

Thanks to Bob Davies, Bobby Wanzer got plenty of open shots. He was one of the NBA's best scorers. In 1951–52, Wanzer became the first player ever to make more than 90 percent of his free throws.

ABOVE: Bob Davies   **RIGHT**: Oscar Robertson

ARNIE RISEN   6´ 9˝ Center

• BORN: 10/9/1924   • PLAYED FOR TEAM: 1947–48 TO 1954–55

Arnie Risen was so tall and skinny that everyone called him "Stilts." He used his long arms and quick feet to drive the NBA's top centers crazy. Risen was elected to the **Hall of Fame** in 1998.

JACK TWYMAN   6´ 6˝ Forward

• BORN: 5/11/1934   • PLAYED FOR TEAM: 1955–56 TO 1965–66

Practice made perfect for Jack Twyman. He rarely went a day without taking hundreds of shots. In 1959–60, Twyman became the first forward in history to average 30 points a game.

OSCAR ROBERTSON   6´ 5˝ Guard

• BORN: 11/24/1938

• PLAYED FOR TEAM: 1960–61 TO 1969–70

Oscar Robertson was big and fast. He had a great head fake and a fade-away jump shot that was impossible to block. Over the course of his first five seasons in the NBA, the "Big O" averaged more than 30 points, 10 assists, and 10 rebounds—in other words, a **triple-double**!

JERRY LUCAS   6´ 8˝ Forward

• BORN: 3/30/1940   • PLAYED FOR TEAM: 1963–64 TO 1969–70

In the late 1960s, Jerry Lucas was the best **all-around** forward in the NBA. He was a great rebounder and had a deadly outside shot. He and Oscar Robertson provided the team with an unstoppable one-two punch.

NATE ARCHIBALD — GUARD

NATE ARCHIBALD   6´ 1˝ **Guard**

- BORN: 9/2/1948
- PLAYED FOR TEAM: 1970–71 TO 1975–76

No one in the NBA could guard Nate Archibald. He could shoot from 25 feet or flash to the basket for a layup. When opponents double-teamed "Tiny," he always found the open man.

MITCH RICHMOND   6´ 5˝ **Guard**

- BORN: 6/30/1965
- PLAYED FOR TEAM: 1991–92 TO 1997–98

Mitch Richmond was one of the few bright spots on the Kings when he played for them. Richmond was a fantastic scorer and a smart, physical defender. Only a handful of guards in history were in his class as an all-around player.

CHRIS WEBBER   6´ 10˝ **Forward/Center**

- BORN: 3/1/1973   • PLAYED FOR TEAM: 1998–99 TO 2004–05

Chris Webber gave the Kings a star they could build a winning team around. He led the NBA in rebounding his first year with Sacramento and averaged 27.1 points per game two seasons later. Webber was a smooth shooter and passer for a player his size.

ABOVE: Nate Archibald
RIGHT: Mike Bibby, Chris Webber, and Peja Stojakovic

PEJA STOJAKOVIC   6´ 9″ Forward

- BORN: 6/9/1977
- PLAYED FOR TEAM: 1998–99 TO 2005–06

Peja Stojakovic was the best shooter in European basketball during the 1990s. He decided to join the NBA and play against the best. The Kings were happy he did. Stojakovic averaged 20 points a game in four different seasons for Sacramento.

MIKE BIBBY   6´ 1″ Guard

- BORN: 5/13/1978
- PLAYED FOR TEAM: 2001–02 TO 2007–08

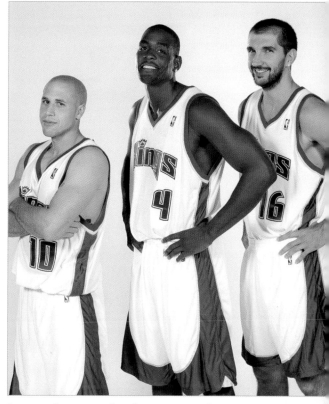

Mike Bibby was one of the NBA's best **clutch** shooters. He wanted the ball with the game on the line. His finest moment came in Game 5 of the 2002 Western Conference Finals. Bibby hit a long shot at the buzzer to beat the Los Angeles Lakers.

KEVIN MARTIN   6´ 7″ Guard

- BORN: 2/1/1983   • FIRST SEASON WITH TEAM: 2004–05

After sitting on the bench as a rookie, Kevin Martin began to earn the trust of his Sacramento teammates. His shooting style seemed strange, but no one could argue with the results. Martin became one of the top scorers in the NBA—and one of the league's best **3-point** shooters.

On the Sidelines

A lot of coaches have come and gone in the 60-plus years since the team began. The man who led the Rochester Royals to three championships in the 1940s and 1950s was Les Harrison. He also owned the team. In 1946–47, Harrison signed an African-American player named Dolly King. It was the beginning of the *integration* of pro basketball.

During the 1960s, Jack McMahon led the Royals. The team won 187 games in four years under him. Later, Bob Cousy coached the Royals. He had won many championships as a player with the Boston Celtics. No matter what Cousy tried—including suiting up for Cincinnati—he could not repeat his success as a coach.

The Kings have had several good coaches since then, including Phil Johnson and Cotton Fitzsimmons. Both were named NBA **Coach of the Year**. Rick Adelman was one of the team's most successful coaches. He led the Kings to the playoffs in each of his eight seasons with the club. In 2007, Sacramento hired Reggie Theus. He felt right at home on the sidelines. Theus had once been a star for the Kings.

Doug Christie gets instructions from Rick Adelman during a 2003–04 game.

One Great Day

When Mitch Richmond's first two shots clanked off the rim at the 1995 NBA All-Star Game, his mind flashed back to a year earlier. At the 1994 All-Star Game, he missed 11 shots. Now Richmond was afraid the nightmare was starting again.

"When I missed those first two," he remembers, "I said to myself, 'Oh no! Not again!'"

It turned out Richmond had nothing to fear. He made 10 of his next 11 shots, including all three of the 3-pointers he tried. Richmond's teammates from the Western Conference were having an even better time than he was—they just kept passing the ball to him and whooping it up every time he swished

a shot. He finished with 23 points in only 22 minutes, as the West beat the East 139–112.

Afterwards, Richmond learned he had been named the game's **Most Valuable Player (MVP)**. It was the perfect end to a great weekend. The Kings had been playing well, and fans were starting to give the team some much-needed respect.

"It felt so good to come and be able to hold my head high, and say 'I'm a Sacramento King,'" Richmond recalls.

Another honor awaited the All-Star MVP when he returned home from the game. The city of Sacramento declared March 1st as Mitch Richmond Day.

Legend Has It

SCOTT WEDMAN ▪ F

Which King was named after a superhero?

LEGEND HAS IT that Scott Wedman was. Wedman—who starred for the Kings during their days in Kansas City—was a health nut. He did not eat meat and spent hour after hour in the gym working on his physique. The Kings called him the "Invisible Hulk" because he was always working out when the other players were out having fun together. In 1979, Wedman was in a terrible car accident. He returned to the court a few games later. Doctors said his strong body had saved him from permanent injuries.

ABOVE: Scott Wedman, the Kings' "Invisible Hulk."
RIGHT: Vlade Divac tries to draw an offensive foul against Shaquille O'Neal.

Which King perfected the art of the offensive foul?

LEGEND HAS IT that Vlade Divac did. An offensive foul is called on a player whose team has the ball. Referees blow the whistle when a player crashes into the man guarding him. Divac learned how to "help" the referees spot offensive fouls by falling to the ground whenever an opponent got too close to him. "I did that because of Shaq," Divac claims, referring to Shaquille O'Neal. "That was the only way to make sure refs called fouls. I had to do that or they would have let him do what he wanted to do."

Which Kings scoring champion was cut three times from his high school team?

LEGEND HAS IT that Nate Archibald was. He attended DeWitt Clinton High School, which had one of the best basketball teams in New York City. Archibald was one of many talented students at the tryouts. After being cut his junior year, the skinny teenager almost quit school. He did the smart thing and stayed. Archibald made the team and became a star in his senior year.

It Really Happened

Maurice Stokes was one of the NBA's best rebounders in the 1950s. He grabbed 38 rebounds in a game during his rookie year. The next season he set a record with 1,256 rebounds.

In the last game of the 1957–58 season, Stokes hit his head on the floor during a game. Three days later, he scored 12 points and hauled in 15 rebounds in a playoff game against the Detroit Pistons. No one could tell, but he was badly hurt.

On the plane ride home, Stokes collapsed. He was rushed to the hospital. Doctors discovered he had a rare form of encephalitis, which is a type of brain injury. Stokes was never able to walk again.

MAURICE STOKES   CINN. Royals

In those days, NBA players did not make a lot of money. The league did not have a plan for taking care of players such as Stokes, either. That is when his best friend and teammate, Jack Twyman, stepped in. Twyman became Big Mo's legal guardian—with the same responsibilities as a parent.

Twyman played in the NBA until 1966. He took care of Stokes until Stokes died of a heart attack at the age of 36. Each summer, NBA players used to gather for the Maurice Stokes Memorial Basketball game, which Twyman started when Stokes was still alive. Now, players participate in a **pro-am** golf tournament for the cause. The money they raise helps other players from pro basketball's early years.

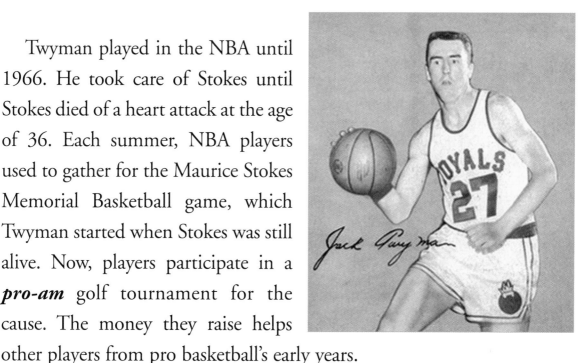

"To this day, I get choked up when I think about what Jack and his family did for Maurice," says teammate Wayne Embry. "It was the ultimate expression of love—what Jack did was one of the best things you'll ever see in pro sports."

How good might the 6′ 7″ Stokes have been had he stayed healthy? He was such an unselfish player that few people outside of Cincinnati realized how many things he did well. "I honestly believe that Maurice had a chance to be perhaps the greatest player of all time," Twyman once said. "He could **legitimately** play forward, guard, or center."

LEFT: A trading card of Maurice Stokes shows him before his brain injury.
ABOVE: Jack Twyman, who shared a lifelong friendship with Stokes.

Team Spirit

Many things have changed in basketball since the team began as the Rochester Royals in the 1940s. However, some things are still the same. Back then, visiting teams did not do well in Rochester's arena. The team's fans were noisy and knowledgeable. They were like a "sixth man"—an extra player who contributed at just the right time.

The same team spirit is alive today in Sacramento. No NBA arena is noisier or more *intimidating* than the Kings' home court. When Sacramento fans aren't cheering for their players, they clap for the Kings Crew hip-hop performers and the Sacramento Kings Dance Team—or SKDT for short. The team's fierce-looking lion *mascot*, Slamson, also keeps the fans entertained.

The Maloof family, which owns the Kings, encourages players to reach out to the fans between games and after each season. Over the years, stars such as Vlade Divac have become as well known off the court as on the court. They take the idea of team spirit to a whole new level.

Gavin Maloof, one of the Kings' owners, and Slamson tell fans which team is #1.

Timeline

The basketball season is played from October through June. That means each season takes place at the end of one year and the beginning of the next. In this timeline, the accomplishments of the Royals and Kings are shown by season.

1950–51
Rochester wins the NBA Championship.

1970–71
Norm Van Lier leads the NBA with 10.1 assists per game.

1945–46
The Royals win the NBL Championship in their first season.

1959–60
Jack Twyman sets a team record with 59 points in a game.

1963–64
Jerry Lucas gets 40 rebounds in a game.

STAR '85

BOB DAVIES
Schick NBA Legends Classic

Bob Davies, the team's first superstar.

Jerry Lucas

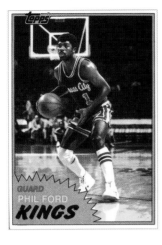

Phil Ford, a leader for the 1978–79 champs.

Mike Bibby

1989–90
Wayman Tisdale makes 15 shots in a row against the Detroit Pistons.

1978–79
The Kings are **Midwest Division** champs.

2006–07
Mike Bibby makes nine 3-pointers in a game.

1980–81
The Kings reach the Western Conference Finals.

1998–99
Chris Webber leads the NBA in rebounding.

2001–02
Sacramento tops the NBA with 61 wins.

Scot Pollard, Bobby Jackson, and Doug Christie celebrate during the 2001–02 season.

Fun Facts

A LITTLE MAGIC

In 1985–86, Reggie Theus had 788 assists for Sacramento. The only other player 6′ 6″ or taller to have that many assists in a season was Magic Johnson (who was 6′ 9″).

HANDS OF STEAL

Sam Lacey had at least 100 blocks and 100 steals six seasons in a row. Only two other centers since then have accomplished this feat—David Robinson and Hakeem Olajuwon.

GOLDEN GUYS

Four players on the 1963–64 Royals had been teammates on the U.S. Olympic team three years earlier. Jerry Lucas, Adrian Smith, Bob Boozer, and Oscar Robertson all won gold medals in Rome, Italy in 1960.

ABOVE: Sam Lacey
RIGHT: A *Webber's World* comic book.

FUNNY BUSINESS

Among Chris Webber's many talents was cartooning. He had his own comic book called *Webber's World*. Its hero was a basketball star who wore number 4.

MINUTE MAN

In 1989–90, Rodney McCray led the NBA with 3,238 minutes played. It is the only time a King has topped the league in that category.

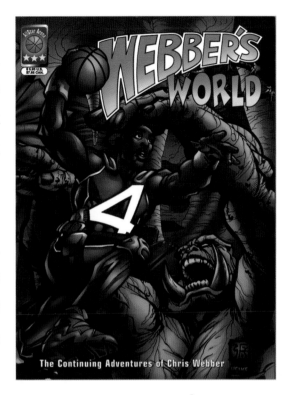

The Continuing Adventures of Chris Webber

ALL THUMBS

Lionel Simmons, one of Sacramento's best players in the 1990s, once went on the injured list because of *tendonitis* in both thumbs. Simmons later admitted he had hurt himself playing video games.

FAMILY TIES

Mike Bibby was a born competitor. His father, Henry, won basketball championships in college and the NBA. His uncle, Jim, was an All-Star baseball pitcher.

Talking Hoops

"I was a rookie, but I wasn't a young basketball player anymore … I had confidence in my knowledge of the game."

—Oscar Robertson, on his first NBA season

"He's one of the best players in this game. He's a superstar."

—Michael Jordan, on Mitch Richmond

"You can't just rely on your athletic ability. You have to grow, you have to learn. You have to have a **zeal** to succeed."

—Wayne Embry, on what it takes to win in the NBA

"It's nice to be in a place that plays through the big guys. You get the opportunity to pass and handle the ball. This is fun."

—Brad Miller, on why he loves playing for the Kings

"Playing basketball has been my dream since I was young and I can't see myself doing anything else."

—Mike Bibby, on realizing his dream of playing in the NBA

"You can do anything. That's the message I want to give. It's about finding something that you love to do, **cultivate** it, work hard at it, and make your life better for you."

—Chris Webber, on setting goals and achieving them

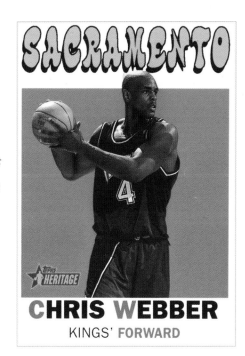

CHRIS WEBBER
KINGS' **FORWARD**

"In my first year, if the man I was guarding scored three straight times, I was taken out. I learned the hard way that you have to challenge the good offensive players."

—Peja Stojakovic, on coming to the NBA from Europe

LEFT: Gavin and Joe Maloof honor Oscar Robertson in February of 2003.
ABOVE: Chris Webber

For the Record

The great Royals and Kings teams and players have left their marks on the record books. These are the "best of the best" …

Red Holzman

Peja Stojakovic

 KINGS AWARD WINNERS

WINNER	AWARD	SEASON
Red Holzman	NBL Rookie of the Year*	1945–46
Les Harrison	NBL Coach of the Year	1945–46
Al Cervi	NBL Most Valuable Player	1946–47
Maurice Stokes	NBA Rookie of the Year	1955–56
Oscar Robertson	NBA All-Star Game MVP	1960–61
Oscar Robertson	NBA Rookie of the Year	1960–61
Oscar Robertson	NBA All-Star Game MVP	1963–64
Jerry Lucas	NBA Rookie of the Year	1963–64
Oscar Robertson	NBA Most Valuable Player	1963–64
Jerry Lucas	NBA All-Star Game MVP	1964–65
Adrian Smith	NBA All-Star Game MVP	1965–66
Oscar Robertson	NBA All-Star Game MVP	1968–69
Phil Johnson	NBA Coach of the Year	1974–75
Phil Ford	NBA Rookie of the Year	1978–79
Cotton Fitzsimmons	NBA Coach of the Year	1978–79
Mitch Richmond	NBA All-Star Game MVP	1994–95
Peja Stojakovic	NBA 3-Point Shootout Champion	2001–02
Peja Stojakovic	NBA 3-Point Shootout Champion	2002–03
Bobby Jackson	NBA Sixth Man of the Year	2002–03

The Rookie of the Year award is given to the league's best first-year player.

KINGS ACHIEVEMENTS

ACHIEVEMENT	SEASON
NBL Champions	1945–46
NBL East Division Champions	1946–47
NBL Champions	1946–47
NBL East Division Champions	1947–48
BAA West Division Champions	1948–49
NBA Central Division co-Champions	1949–50
NBA Champions	1950–51
NBA West Division Champions	1951–52
NBA Midwest Division Champions	1978–79
NBA Pacific Division Champions	2001–02
NBA Pacific Division Champions	2002–03

OSCAR ROBERTSON
guard

CINCINNATI

LEFT: An autographed photo of Bob Davies, the star of Rochester's NBL championship teams.
ABOVE: Oscar Robertson, Cincinnati's best player during the 1960s.

Pinpoints

The history of a basketball team is made up of many smaller stories. These stories take place all over the map—not just in the city a team calls "home." Match the push-pins on these maps to the Team Facts and you will begin to see the story of the Kings unfold!

TEAM FACTS

1 Sacramento, California—*The Kings have played here since the 1985–86 season.*

2 Inglewood, California—*Reggie Theus was born here.*

3 Tulsa, Oklahoma—*Wayman Tisdale was born here.*

4 Indianola, Mississippi—*Sam Lacey was born here.*

5 Detroit, Michigan—*Chris Webber was born here.*

6 Charlotte, Tennessee—*Oscar Robertson was born here.*

7 Indianapolis, Indiana—*Tom Van Arsdale was born here.*

8 Middletown, Ohio—*Jerry Lucas was born here.*

9 Rochester, New York—*The team played here as the Royals from 1945–46 to 1956–57.*

10 New York, New York—*Nate Archibald was born here.*

11 Fort Lauderdale, Florida—*Mitch Richmond was born here.*

12 Belgrade, Yugoslavia*—*Peja Stojakovic was born here.*

Yugoslavia is now known as Serbia.

Reggie Theus

Play Ball

Basketball is a sport played by two teams of five players. NBA games have four 12-minute quarters—48 minutes in all—and the team that scores the most points when time has run out is the winner. Most baskets count for two points. Players who make shots from beyond the three-point line receive an extra point. Baskets made from the free-throw line count for one point. Free throws are penalty shots awarded to a team, usually after an opponent has committed a foul. A foul is called when one player makes hard contact with another.

Players can move around all they want, but the player with the ball cannot. He must bounce the ball with one hand or the other (but never both) in order to go from one part of the court to another. As long as he keeps "dribbling," he can keep moving.

In the NBA, teams must attempt a shot every 24 seconds, so there is little time to waste. The job of the defense is to make it as difficult as possible to take a good shot—and to grab the ball if the other team shoots and misses.

This may sound simple, but anyone who has played the game knows that basketball can be very complicated. Every player on the court has a job to do. Different players have different strengths and weaknesses. The coach must mix these players in just the right way, and teach them to work together as one.

The more you play and watch basketball, the more "little things" you are likely to notice. The next time you are at a game, look for these plays:

PLAY LIST

ALLEY-OOP—A play where the passer throws the ball just to the side of the rim—so a teammate can catch it and dunk in one motion.

BACK-DOOR PLAY—A play where the passer waits for his teammate to fake the defender away from the basket—then throws him the ball when he cuts back toward the basket.

KICK-OUT—A play where the ball-handler waits for the defense to surround him—then quickly passes to a teammate who is open for an outside shot. The ball is not really kicked in this play; the term comes from the action of pinball machines.

NO-LOOK PASS—A play where the passer fools a defender (with his eyes) into covering one teammate—then suddenly passes to another without looking.

PICK-AND-ROLL—A play where one teammate blocks or "picks off" another's defender with his body—then cuts to the basket for a pass in the confusion.

Glossary

3-POINT—A shot taken from behind the 3-point line.

ALL-AROUND—Good at all parts of the game.

ALL-STARS—Players selected to play in the annual All-Star Game.

ASSISTS—Passes that lead to successful shots.

BASKETBALL ASSOCIATION OF AMERICA (BAA)—The professional league that started in 1946–47 and later became the NBA.

CLUTCH—Able to perform well under pressure.

COACH OF THE YEAR—An award given each season to the league's best coach.

DIVISION—A group of teams within a league that play in the same part of the country.

HALL OF FAME—The museum in Springfield, Massachusetts where basketball's greatest players are honored. A player voted into the Hall of Fame is sometimes called a "Hall of Famer."

LINEUP—The list of players who are playing in a game.

MIDWEST DIVISION—A division for teams that play in the central part of the country.

MINOR LEAGUES—The many professional baseball leagues that help develop players for the major leagues.

MOST VALUABLE PLAYER (MVP)—The award given each year to the league's best player; also given to the best player in the league finals and All-Star Game.

NATIONAL BASKETBALL ASSOCIATION (NBA)—The professional league that has been operating since 1946–47.

NATIONAL BASKETBALL LEAGUE (NBL)—An early professional league that played 12 seasons, from 1937–38 to 1948–49, then merged with the Basketball Association of America to become the NBA.

OVERTIME—The extra period played when a game is tied after 48 minutes.

PLAYMAKERS—Players who help their teammates score by passing the ball.

PLAYOFFS—The games played after the season to determine the league champion.

PROFESSIONAL—A player or team that plays a sport for money. College players are not paid, so they are considered "amateurs."

ROLE PLAYERS—People who are asked to do specific things when they are in a game.

ROOKIE—A player in his first season.

SUBSTITUTE—A player who begins most games on the bench.

TRIPLE-DOUBLE—A game in which a player records double-figures in three different statistical categories.

WESTERN CONFERENCE FINALS—The playoff series that determines which team from the West will play the best team in the East for the NBA Championship.

WOMEN'S NATIONAL BASKETBALL ASSOCIATION (WNBA)—The professional league for women that started in 1996.

OTHER WORDS TO KNOW

BURLY—Having a large, strong body.

CENTURY—A period of 100 years.

CULTIVATE—Develop.

DECADE—A period of 10 years; also specific periods, such as the 1950s.

INTEGRATION—The act of bringing people of different races and backgrounds into one group.

INTIMIDATING—Scary or frightening.

LEGITIMATELY—Having reached a standard judged favorably by everyone.

LOGO—A symbol or design that represents a company or team.

MASCOT—An animal or person believed to bring a group good luck.

PRO-AM—An event in which professionals and amateurs participate.

SATIN—A smooth, shiny fabric.

SYNTHETIC—Made in a laboratory, not in nature.

TENDONITIS—Swelling of the tissue that connects muscles to other parts of the body.

TRADITION—A belief or custom that is handed down from generation to generation.

UPHOLD—To maintain or give support.

ZEAL—Passion or excitement.

Places to Go

ON THE ROAD

SACRAMENTO KINGS
One Sports Parkway
Sacramento, California 95834
(916) 928-0000

NAISMITH MEMORIAL BASKETBALL HALL OF FAME
1000 West Columbus Avenue
Springfield, Massachusetts 01105
(877) 4HOOPLA

ON THE WEB

THE NATIONAL BASKETBALL ASSOCIATION   www.nba.com
  • *Learn more about the league's teams, players, and history*

THE SACRAMENTO KINGS   www.nba.com/kings
  • *Learn more about the Kings*

THE BASKETBALL HALL OF FAME   www.hoophall.com
  • *Learn more about history's greatest players*

ON THE BOOKSHELF

To learn more about the sport of basketball, look for these books at your library or bookstore:

  • Hareas, John. *Basketball*. New York, New York: DK, 2005.

  • Hughes, Morgan. *Basketball*. Vero Beach, Florida: Rourke Publishing, 2005.

  • Thomas, Keltie. *How Basketball Works*. Berkeley, California: Maple Tree Press, distributed through Publishers Group West, 2005.

Index

PAGE NUMBERS IN **BOLD** REFER TO ILLUSTRATIONS.

The Team

MARK STEWART has written more than 20 books on basketball, and over 100 sports books for kids. He grew up in New York City during the 1960s rooting for the Knicks and Nets, and now takes his two daughters, Mariah and Rachel, to watch them play. Mark comes from a family of writers. His grandfather was Sunday Editor of *The New York Times* and his mother was Articles Editor of *The Ladies Home Journal* and *McCall's*. Mark has profiled hundreds of athletes over the last 20 years. He has also written several books about his native New York, and New Jersey, his home today. Mark is a graduate of Duke University, with a degree in history. He lives with his daughters and wife, Sarah, overlooking Sandy Hook, New Jersey.

MATT ZEYSING is the resident historian at the Basketball Hall of Fame in Springfield, Massachusetts. His research interests include the origins of the game of basketball, the development of professional basketball in the first half of the twentieth century, and the culture and meaning of basketball in American society.